A
HIGH-SPIRITED
WOMAN

A
High-Spirited
Woman

Carol Meredith

A High-Spirited Woman
Copyright ©2017 Carol Meredith

ISBN: 978-1-940769-79-0
Publisher: Mercury HeartLink
Printed in the United States of America

Contact: *desertathome@yahoo.com*

Mercury HeartLink
www.heartlink.com

front cover art "Serenity"
by Kenneth Rougeau

kennethrougeau.com

Contents

A
HIGH-SPIRITED
WOMAN

DEDICATION

This collection of poetry must be dedicated to both my life's most long-enduring and forever loves who have lifted and sustained me throughout my life both in joyful and painful times, to my loving daughter Jessica, kind and good in every way and a treasure each day of my life, and to the everlasting memory of my Grandmother Hazel Evelyn, a beloved woman special in every way I could ever understand and those ways I can only appreciate more as time travels on, and to my newest one, Leland, a grandson who came into our lives through profound faith of things believed but not seen-that is, until he appeared. My dearest wish is that he will grow courageously throughout life to know his special uniqueness and to derive joy at each bend in the road, continue to experience beauty and goodness and that he will always feel the love that surrounds him on earth and in heavenly realms. I pray he will always feel the depth and breadth of my endless, forever and ever love for him.

I also dedicate this work and acknowledgement of my teachers from first grade through graduate school, each gifted to share their passion, knowledge, and inspired teaching with their many students throughout the years. They certainly changed the world.

From the Land of Enchantment
in the Year of our Lord 2017

To The Reader

Poetry is perhaps one of the most personal writing that one may attempt. One cannot hide inside its words. It goes to the core of all human emotions where it finds expression and flows unashamedly from that passionate connection. It is the sound of the poet's soul that often finds its voice midst the storms of life where uncertainties live. It demands that its author write the words, and in that way enters the world from the realm of the ethereal. Hopefully its existence will reach into the thoughts and experiences of the reader and find a response with the author's words. Inspiration travels by many tributaries and finds its destination as it was always intended. Poetry is likely one of the greatest examples of inspiration at work. At its conception we believe in its merit and go forward, not knowing where that work will find new roots and bloom on its own. We only know that it connects us in almost magical ways.

Gray Magic

We meet in the past now
the same two we were in the
beginning before the war
gave back fathers, brothers,
strangers long before time
began moving backward
in broken rhythm

Word for word we knew
the other's world.
It was not easy to miss
looking into almost the
same face, sharing one voice
singing into the hymnal page,
the verses lost in the closeness
of exact time

Deftly, surely, the thinnest cracks
splayed strong brick-years,
shifting friends and places in
the mortal quake, "Is Mary dead?"
again she asks, her face a mask
of innocent unknowing

In the soft, slippery
here-and-now, the old path
was ready, never doubting
this moment would come
its latticed memory matted deep
in blackest soil

And time's dried quilt eagerly lifts
to show what is sleeping there,
protected, unharmed, eternal.
Einstein-time runs true,
fulfilled in its premise,
its theory proven so simply
that it makes perfect sense
to a person without a drop
of physics in the blood

Suspended, like floating flecks
of dust rotating on ribbons of
sunlight we know where we are,
the landscape of our lives
crystalline clear

We laugh at the old stories
precision-made, unchanging
while the bluest blue sky
shifts its billows we look on
the same world and remember
every word, each long-spending
memory of love

Branches and Parts

The rain, already fallen,
still moves in the street.
The droplets make no noise
except when a car goes by
and flattens their fat,
joyous bodies

Then and only then,
a sizzle leaps at the tire
but never wins

So final to hear dying rain
trying to retain some part
of what has been theirs
from a preordained and
mighty fall

REUNION

"I've come one last time,"
she said, her voice not as
I'd remembered it but
of course that was years
ago in another world

Different, yet the same,
now holding the fading
image of youth in place of
the high promise of
womanhood

she didn't seem to recognize
me and I, embarrassed
not hurt, remembered my
pride so dearly paid
on that other long ago day

Fateful how we have
come together holding
such fragile memories
with paper plates but we
always were the ones

to recognize the paradoxes
and sharing so much more
than we knew then

My fantasy all these years
had been to hear her say
"I'm sorry, I'm sorry,"
but in all fairness my needs
have been changing
for a long time now

The stories must be true,
he left her as he once left me
for her and as we embrace
I hear myself say
"I'm sorry, I'm sorry"

Liberation in New Orleans

My snow mind plays
pitch and catch in
yesterday's field while
others have flown
the earth with the ease
of stone words

Should the memory
not last long enough
to satisfy immortality
surely reason will
be gentleman enough
to rescue it
and silver-tongued
clever to gain favor
for its remains

OUTSIDE THE BELL-SHAPED CURVE

Unanxiously she moves
among her peers
happily unaware that she
should be otherwise, not knowing
one-out-of-four cancer fears

She never knew a Philip Slater
was he playing downtown?
or that it's urban renewal moving
panther like through the city
making it purposely brown

A pity, they say, her innocence
has been so poorly spent
that her values keep her prisoner
in a body and mind not meant
for more but less

A pity, they say, our Great Society
permits her tricks
and so it must seem to them
passionately wedged among
tons of white-washed bricks

Later on as trembling lights
beckon a few,
she'll go unafraid
up some half-wide street
into a building that probably
was never new
and on a couch where cushions
separate not meet,
become a dreamer of all
but nightmares

VIEW FROM THE TRAIN

We sat there, marble-eyed
and waiting
but the scene didn't wait
or slow its gaiting. Uncoiling
like a spring undone
my mind bounded with the train
until it seemed I was lost
in my thoughts as small
as sparkles of rain
I looked around me
and saw others who seemed
left behind by unceasing motion,
whose faces were bare
of all except their self
for the windows, cut by
sharp silver lines stop
any thought and I knew
I too must resign myself
to my face, the only still
thing. Strange how you can
see through your face on a train,

see the patternless picture
of all running fast
knowing not even the blur
will last

SOMEWHERE IN NEW MEXICO

Somewhere in New Mexico
night dances on
oblivious to what can only be
spirits whining to reclaim
their lost memory

Dust devils, determined
to make festive ruffles
of the shrill meet warning
in the glow of the Kiva's belly
as frayed legends hover
in orange smoke,
storytellers hushed
longing to speak

But nowhere does the moonrise
find a shadow that will name
its own firstborn and night,
heady as an impudent child,
swirls headlong into
immortality's yearning arms

clueless
christened by stars
baptized by wind
motherless

Bourbon Street Wake-Up Call

Morning is on the streets
still wearing a sleepy face,
night not quite gone
waiting to be dumped
rests in plastic bags
and sits on red-cobbled,
hosed-down sidewalks
but pristine
they're not

Smells run from the water,
from the leftovers of the night
from the oversize dogs
that saunter, grunt,
let it all go
here on Bourbon Street
makes quite a sight
but distasteful
it's not

So I've made up my mind,
if I have to die, if I have to go
then I'll live with that unkind

turn of events, but give me
some creative leeway
on the other side,

just let the call come straightaway
from the French Quarter's guide,
where I can recognize the
the golden purr of a low-bellied
trumpet voice, my own Gideon's,
calling me to "wake up, wake up"
his amber reflection winging me home
right here on Bourbon Street

Bitter Water

At last the beginning is
over and rejoicing comes
gratefully, a hallelujah with
benediction
Longing to know from
inside out the vast
you has pulled at my
consciousness and kept me
from being free

But more than knowing
I have wanted to be
free of needing to know,
my own thoughts
making me captive
not of love's question mark
but of my own mind

Still, I must allow for your
resistance to superficial
truth which comes
easily from wafer-thin
people

They say you can drown
just as easily
in shallow water

Up From Nowhere

She was selling insurance
looking at me she asked
how long he'd been dead.
A long time, I told her
I was nineteen
now I'm thirty-three.
She reassured me
I didn't look my age

All at once she remembered
things she herself thought
she'd forgotten
The past was suddenly
pregnant with possible
connections between us,
and Leakey would have
been proud to learn
my dead father was part
of the missing link

Public Assistance and Love

They pass through my door,
like perfected characters
known only to omniscient authors
faces stamped to the bone
with hope used up but yet
again, they must ask

They ask a favor I cannot
grant, not because I wouldn't
but because their need doesn't
match and the gap is too great
for them to survive the divide
where nothing fits

There is it seems no program
for renewal of the shattered soul,
no rehab for life's wayward ways

Giving the answer in the manual,
quoting chapter and verse from
the bible of the down-and-out
eyes drain down pale cheeks,
making sad rivers that spill over

into chins waiting to ripple,
all the while dripping as if
Dali himself had stroked
their face, melting down
insides into a raw landscape
of dispirited time

A Long Line of High-Spirited Women

Fortunately my heritage claims a long
line of high-spirited women, truly free
before women were supposed to be

Their horses were fast, ready to carry them
away from chores and men and lifeless lives
draining their spirits with butter knives

Birth marked with sprigs of the Quaker heart
wildly growing in mind and soul, pleading
to go where truth could sprout its seedlings

My bloodline flows with passionate questions
ready to burst free of veins, claiming first rights
to all in me, as sirens sing back-to-back bytes

My soul hears the unsung words while I
feel my feet begin to move down another road
with new hope new joy, and seeds to be sown

TRIBUTE TO WALLACE STEVENS

The burning bush of knowledge
found itself a charcoal image
in abandoned halls of former truth

But words lingered, hanging onto
bits of dust hidden in the old air,
fast glimpsed only when
perfect sun revealed them there,
and words became symbols again,
like great strings of flickering
lights keeping vigil

Delicately at first they sparked against
each other, finally glowing fast
down the long narrow oak halls
splitting the darkness apart

And then silence. The hallways joined
the charcoal in its memory and most
who recognized the ashes feared
the lights, too, were gone

Non-glare buildings rose easily
from the gray ground and cold lights
seemed to ignite themselves overnight
but in one hallway some had been
reached with a warmth
that kept marking its glowing
path down the chiseled
chrome hallways

And the warmth lasted, its medium
lighting the way, held carefully
among time's chill

THE BEST FOR LAST

Why do they always say
"the best has been saved for last?"

I know
that just isn't so
and so do you
if you're honest, if you're willing
to face it

The circling wheelchairs
know and close ranks
looking for something lost
they draw inward while
eyes sweep the floor
with lips silenced by
strokes' frivolous mime
as memories mutter their own
unintelligible, inglorious story
propaganda's mistress
hums along

Staring back from somewhere
mockery made of brighter days

truth-pimped lies whatsoever for?
life gone missing in action?
no more than time's trickster
whore
not so alluring anymore

We know whatever the best was
to be has already been
we just didn't know it then,

and what's left is only just that
nothing golden yet to be
promised but not granted
to you and me

PENTIMENTO

The night of March 13 just so
happened was Friday the thirteenth
but no special reason that the
dream would have come as it did
that night because the dream was
anything but foreboding or scary
No, not that
It was beautiful so much that it
had to be preserved in daylight.
It was so clear, not that the meaning
was clear for it surely was not
but all the elements of truth
and blissful senses were bright stars
in my dream that skipped backward
to long ago, but not so long I guess
if it could be that unmistakable to me

In the dream I am walking in my
small hometown, going toward
where the schools cluster and as I
got closer to what my destination
must have been, I was given a ride
by my middle school geography

teacher, of whom I was fond
In my dream I was grown and he was
the same as he was in the classroom.
Both adults, we talked little pleasantries
and I noticed we were moving
north past the schools and there not
far ahead was an unexpectedly
beautiful view where once grassy
pastures and lazy, untended grains grew
now elegant homes hugged the land,
large, multi-level with windows
dazzling as if crossed sword blades
were striking each other making
the streets brighter than any sun
ever could have
Palmettos fluttered on the greener
than green lawns in what seemed
to be joyful southwest winds
Because my hometown sits in the very
Midwestern heartland, this was an
unexpected reality, but I accepted the
mystical addition to my quaint town
without question because

it pleased me beyond anything!
What progress I think I thought
in this place of great sameness.
How did it happen?
The dream was long, engaging me,
finding no need to end and unlike
most of my dreams,
I didn't know I was dreaming
I was there feeling with my flesh,
living what was happening as it
happened without any strangeness
at what it showed me

The dream lingered, that happy breeze
touched my skin, sensing the perfect
balance of it all and I wondered,
what did it mean?

But nothing came to me then or now
and I must wonder if it's a glimpse
of what heaven is or could be if we're
lucky, a place where the many mansions
are built to the blueprint in our heart,

a place we know so well, where we see
and hear those dear ones, the ones we've
known who will also love us in a dream
without end? The peace I felt was
complete, and I wonder

SOMEONE TO CRY WITH

Whatever happened
to Marlene Petrovich?
Did she finally find a foolproof way
to hide among the trail
of heartaches she once openly
Native style as her lips
sent perfect smoke rings
to smack that dirty cracked ceiling?
Looking back I don't think I was
necessary to her sad laments
of lost lovers and such things,
but silently applauded her
bravado, false or not
and it was understood
the half-moon bra was necessary
to socially connect, its padded
reality busy catching the onslaught
of crystal tears as she suffered
through a watery nose

Whatever happened to those other ghosts,
those two we thought we were?
when the smallest thing was the

biggest thing, feeling your eyes
fold into mine as our lives touched
Olympic ice, flying bright and free
scoring top-of-the-mark happy
from every mundane atom until some
random, lethal chance shifted reality
like an earthquake overturning
itself where time's lava runs without
aim, smolders and finally spits
itself out among its sad coals
letting you know for sure you're
alone
needing someone to cry with

THE SEA FAERIE SPEAKS

The sea faerie speaks
early in the morning
when I'm showering
It seems to be her favorite
time to tantalize me
as the water sprays
she speaks
The things she says are
unbelievable, yet I want
to believe them
so I keep listening.
Only today she told me I should
change my direction
Can you imagine?
Her exact words were
"You can swim further out
if you want to"

When she speaks I'm sure
she's right
I'm sure she knows
But speaking to me
in the mornings isn't enough.

I need to hear her all day long
and boldly interrupt my dreams
at night, enough for me to
believe and start the long
journey to where the land
disappears

Prayers of The Grandmothers

You ask why they are the ones given
the torch to transfuse this otherworldly
love journeying through the gray haze
of uncertain time placing their hearts'
marrow into the new souls
You can ask but an answer you will
understand cannot be given, no
simple answer that makes the long
past and all tomorrows bind together
like a book picked up and read one
rainy afternoon, never that
the brain has no way to recognize
infinite anything because it cannot
enter limitless time. It only knows
the word. The living motherlode
blood of immortality alone can carry it,
a fountainhead flowing untouched by
worldly taint or man's mortal poison
where holiness lives free, unchanged
as it has been and as it shall be
Before the soul dreams its first breath
the ritual of perfect passion has cast
love's purest bond into the unborn

from the grandmothers' cup of endless time
and those same ones who may never have
heard that voice speak for their own now
speak loudly, eloquently for the new
children they claim, these guardians,
the incarnate vessel chosen before time
ordained to carry the precious spiriting
spring, its natural purpose to stay forever
and a day with the beloved
children of the children of the children
Armed from their fortress with voices
lifted against a world's ugly truths,
they stand ready their hearts beating
as one with the children who need them,
clutching drops of mystical purity, tears of
their own souls' eternal purpose that fill
again and again the protected reservoir,
and come to life as the grandmothers
pray

Hell Into Earth

He stood there, eyes stinging,
trying to see what he could not
know, where was he?
How had he come to this place?
His tiny body quivered,
seeing nothing, knowing nothing
Tiny lungs filled with devil's smoke
and smoke of others he did not
remember, the most tender of soul bodies
filled with poison beaten into his five
tiny pounds until his brain dizzied with
toxic blood of the damned he had come
to the edge of something What?

Knowing not backward nor
forward the way anywhere,
what could he do?
Something in his breast
began to move faster and faster
just a moment ago he was a
dreamer in a sleepless sleep
where faces were only sad feelings,
and now the faintest hope

sparked something he could not
know yet but across time
and space he had come
searching, somehow knowing
he had chosen to leave this
place for another, the little
frightened soul made his way
across Eternity's divide

The Circus Mistress

The circus came to the little town
led faithfully by tumbling clowns
the railroad made sure of it

Young and old loved the sparkling shows
high-flying wire walkers' agile toes
and fortune tellers knowing all

The robust, flashy circus master
whipped the lions, courted disaster
and had another thought or two

One day a tiny, black-eyed lady
stepped onto the platform, ready
to see the town through his fiery eyes

Down the way, he freely took her arm
seeming under a spell so charmed
by each other and the grand idea

The house he built had lace gingerbread
with scallops from the porch overhead
and fantasy spirals all around

Her adoring eyes glistened with tears
the home she longed for at last hers
and his when the circus was in town

The people of this church-going place
shunned her, never looking on her face
with lowered eyes they crossed the street

All of them knew who and what she was
gossip grew fiercer and mean because
she was not welcome in their town

The circus train came less and less
someone said it now went further west
and gaiety soon followed its tracks

She walked among them one last time
down lovely streets where trees grew lined
and the friendly little town watched her go

A TOUCH OF EDYTHE

There were so many things about her
an original to be sure but you could never
quite put your finger on it, the truth was
she was absolutely irresistible to the
opposite sex with a mystique stretching from
years before Pearl Harbor to long after the
Viet Nam era exhaled its last deep sigh
Of course there were the husbands,
and a stream of smitten men, although
no one knows the count, some old enough
to be her father, others young enough to be
her son, one who threw public tantrums,
threatening suicide if she ever "left" him
Tall and slender with a pleasant enough
face but nothing more, a conservative, plain
dresser never drawing attention to herself,
it was something else she possessed hidden
from any blood work or ancestry DNA
markers, something that could not be named
atavistic perhaps, alive centuries ago when
each human emitted a unique essence, potent
and honest before bodily adornment or wiles

to attract another existed, its own natural
magic, pure and innocent, no longer a part
of us

People who knew her all her life kept
trying to figure her out but no clues were
ever found, just the same no one could
seem to forget her, women wanting
what she had and men just wanting her

Breaking of The Bread

Purposely she waited another day or two
before she carried it to the browning yard
now easy to crumble, the dry bread would do

Under a painter's perfect sky of paling blue
she surveyed her small kingdom and smiled
at another innocent day coming true

Lifting her eyes she saw, sitting perfectly still
on the wires overhead, her quiet companions
waiting, ready to join her in this sacred will

Her palms open, soft wind carried the dust
over the ground now holy, the bread broken
for them and for her from each tiny crust

Moravian Nights

"Sweet dreams, my darling child,"
she said to the fluttering eyelids
as she pulled the covers up
just touching the tiny chin

She knew the child was fighting fear,
she felt it falling through the air
she breathed everywhere
but she knew the child was safe

"The angels are always here" she said
caressing the child's warm forehead
"All night they stand by your bed
stretching feathery wings over you"

"Your angels never need to sleep" she
whispered to the nearly-dozing child
whose peaceful face now softly smiled
"this holy place is their earthly home"

She was sure as she turned to leave
an embrace made of a fluttering breeze

held her close, so tender and dear
and an almost remembered lullaby
sat still on her memory like a
butterfly

Country Music and Soul Food

Primitive sounds eat unashamed
at the heart's door, feeding
what is cavernous there
what remembers the past
craving what will last
keeping itself ready in a new
dress with a fresh face
just in case
and the same heart hears
the soul of banquet nights
where everyone wins
where those
medal of honor wearers,
man o' the year
man o' war
triple crown steeds
gold metal finalists
proud Oscar-holders
and blue-ribbon bearers
wear golden globe smiles
all of them out there
just beyond the footlights
somewhere in those crowded

rooms of the wistful hearted
waiting to hear, waiting
listening to the melody of
truth and circumstance

Under the Cumberland Falls

Water falls heavily polishing grayed stone
slabs slick from high overhead where
beauty and danger, birthright conspirators
know one droplet could be the pellet
of death if it dropped at just the right
moment on this precipice of
imminent domain, if her foot slipped
or his, dragging the other into the rush.
Unholy words spewed from his lips,
preaching a damnation of their love,
repeating threats of quick mortality
mimicking the fall's menacing gush
as it emptied endlessly above them
bouncing innocent-looking foam onto
the rocks underfoot. Devil-blue eyes
condemn her but by now her fear had
hardened itself, transforming into an
engine pumping sludge from her
spirit as the blacksmith of her soul
raised glistening arms to beat mighty
wings of steel to rest beneath her,
now her own warrior like David,
faced the enemy with only the

shield of a pure heart knowing
when the sun sets on this day she
would be free one way or another
even if by her own death

As Death swirled around her, she felt
her mother's eyes come alive in hers
then burn into her towering enemy and
made a vow of forever that rose above
the water's roar. Staring up into her
long ago love she gave the requiem
"Do it now or forget all that has been
between us. It is over." Then she turned,
her foot finding the next water-carved
rock and cautiously walked away

Keeping the Peace

The voice said she called too often, the
words falling like snow on the sunniest
of days, melting the phone with a click

there was no reason for her to call again
they said unless he was trying to hurt her
then she should call and they would come

every cell of her thin body knew he would
craving the closeness of her more than ever
lusting to plunge a knife in her beating heart

they refused to look at his tormented madness
that's for doctors they said and could not
understand why or how she knew it so well

entering the labyrinth of his hate-riddled
soul was the only way she knew to survive
and all these years had kept her body alive

now the fallen angel was loose, an unleashed
mad dog, waiting to beat down the door
in love with keeping his unholy promise

she knew there was no hope she could have,
still life seeks itself even after hope has left
thinking a miracle could still happen, maybe

The last call was short and pointless, they did
not even hear the voice of life and death
staining into the shabby indoor-outdoor carpet

wordlessly she kept the peace and
hung up the phone

Holy Rollers

My second cousin Bill
on my mother's side was
born again before he died

He talked in tongues, prayed
long prayers, the kind that
brings to life miracle things

The only problem was in
the here-and now when he
lost his first life he also
lost his first wife

Religion played the ill-suited
heavy but so well-fated
an odd ménage a trios
while the obvious waited

She called them holy-rollers
not her kind of church-goers
knowing what was to be done
she sent him packing for one

Her next husband, issues-ridden
wanted her savings in his name
not her kids, foolishly she
submitted and did his bidding

Everything turned rotten then
love not able to sit or stand
in the rubble of nothing so
she dissolved them too in court

When Bill finally died at last
long after the drama was gone
his first wife, I heard, dissolved
in a tear or two of her own past

REFUSE

Garbage and marriage
go together
just see them there
it's like clockwork

First it looks cozily
pre-arranged
hardly ever changing
but garbage grows

Recycling might work
for some but not
well enough for those
with the wrong "stuff"

Dumping into others' bins
is risky and needs night
as much as grit
but there's always more

More and more every day
until burning weeks' worth
of living looks promising
even if it smells bad

Marriage and garbage
match the needs of each
without knowing they may
so easily bring out the worst

August

A different air moves through the leaves
and once again, they seem uneasy
knowing when August leaves, they will
go wherever the wind decides

Even the dirt underfoot flies in the air
rising, blowing itself away to the time of year
has a different call than yesterday
not quite afraid yet wary of something

High above single-engine planes cut
through the sky without noticing their voice
is another kind of whirr now, leaving sounds
that carry a trail of soft longing to the ground

Birds search for each other as they must leave
soon even if they would rather stay they will
follow one that will lead them to their next
home, the choice not theirs, still they go

County fairs must wait for another year
to bring bites of cotton candy and elephant
ears while the Ferris wheel grease congeals,
young and old and birds of the air yearn
and pray for an early Spring

Invisible

In many ways she had always been alone
her family not missing the sadness
but none of what they thought they knew
helped her, she was left to love pills and sleep,
needing more as the days passed

The son and daughter who filled her space
seemed to vaporize as she sat, patting
expensive creams onto her face
and looking deep into herself that day,
something inside just gave way

Her husband, ready to do whatever he
could for the woman he loved, was at
his wit's end and took her to get her hair
done, thinking it would brighten the day
and it did, or seemed to for a time

When her legs stopped walking
he carried her from the bed to the
sofa each morning, arranging her like
a favorite doll with a cracked smile

and carried her to the hairdresser
and to the psychiatrist

Try as he might, the doctor could find
nothing amiss with this perfectly coiffed
fifty-something woman and when the
husband asked why she could not walk
the psychiatrist said "It's all in her head"

Stuck in her ever-pulling quicksand world,
it just might be she couldn't pretend
one day longer that everything was all
right and took to her bed, loving pills
and long dreamless sleep

WHAT WOULD YOU DO

Thrown to the wind
caution knew what to do
and tossed it back
without a second glance

REDEMPTION

Randomly placed and spread so thin
her own brand of semi-precious sin
seemed unlikely to redeem itself,
leaving her hollowed out like a
bamboo flute

So, she blew into it letting herself
imagine all sorts of things good and
bad thinking it might even give her
a way out of a tangled life web,
magically overriding wrong for right
at the sounds her fingers made

She believed in sanctity, and tried
to find the answer while Understanding
stood aloof fluttering like a frantic
hummingbird as she played what
seemed only foolish tunes

Not aware of the darkened orchestra
around her she laid down the flute
and heard a hesitant melody that
seemed missing a part between bars

In a way she could not understand
she began to feel less alone
and not sure why
picked up the flute again

Wearing the faintest smile of hope
she thought there might be others
like her if only in her mind
and they might need to hear her
and know she was there

In My Mother's House

In my Mother's house memory
is a Queen very much alive, one
who has more than a strong scepter
she has great wisdom that sits
easily under her enormous
studded crown

That wisdom does not forget the
smallest tear or the longest hurt of
teenage years because growing up
is the hardest thing yet must be
done. Talk can seem cheap
when it comes from those already
grown up into their own world

Yet when the older others speak, it
is with a voice that sounds like they
know something, as though living
such a long time has given their
words wings of inner reckoning
and fewer words can speak greater
influence pulling comfort near
even when it is something the
younger do not want to hear

In my Mother's house, ghosts tell
everything, sometimes they whisper
sometimes they shout the secrets so
loudly they're no longer secrets
and tears can, at last, be dried

In my Daughter's house, again safe
from the world's uncaring sadness
that sits tapping long fingers,
impatient for tomorrow's many torrents
to come calling

as the rain starts to rush hard at the
double pane windows, trying to
frighten us all with prize punches
of thunder loud enough to wake
the little ones, that child of long ago
knows what to do

The grass will sparkle gloriously
in the daylight and the young will
not remember waking up in the night
or why Grandma was in their bed
this morning, but they will be glad

No Naaman No

Go, Naaman, go! Wash yourself
in the River Jordan and your
deepest wish will be granted

You, Assyrian General that you are
Take this order! Do it now! Don't wait!
What pride keeps you so sure
of yourself in battle yet deathly afraid
of the truth without a sword?
What mania dares show its face
while you suffer?

Loosen your robes, Naaman
Let them fall away like your rotting flesh
while you walk into the healing waters
and be made whole once again

No Ordinary Moments

No ordinary moments there were
that went between us, just exquisite ones
from a generator pulsating from
beating hearts, recharging without
hesitancy or thought, only longing
for that moment and the next

women's magazines write so
boldly about wisdom in waiting
to choose a lifelong mate, but I fear
those authors know little what
I know from my soul's sadness
that choosing is not always
choice but may be divinity trying
to tell you something about trusting
what you cannot understand

It is a hard-borne truth to learn
when knowing can no longer matter
because it is far too late
and all your moments are sinfully,
eternally horribly ordinary,
ones you would never have chosen
in a million years

THE FAIR

Dirt underfoot marks the spot
where it all comes to life, magic
ensues and eyes sparkle in the dusk
along with the almost Christmas kind of
lights of the happily-moving Ferris Wheel
bringing the bright moon down to them

Children know this time is special and
belongs to them as parents look on,
bored with it all, already forgotten
how magic works anyway,
the sweet taste of it wrapped in
sugary stealth that melts
so heavenly on the child's tongue
while the carousel music calls
them near, the little ones want
only for this to never end
and the parents want only
for the last ride to be over
and the lights to dim

But the children smile to themselves
hugging the truth close
knowing the fair will come again
next year and they will be there

PINK OPALS

Beautiful buds of the earth they
search for you, high, high in the
Andes where strangers must struggle
for even the most shallow breath,
where the sky draws down to touch
these peaks, obscuring those who
quietly sit in reverent openness
to the Universe's stillness, waiting
for the voice that alone will guide them
without maps or man's technology
they meditate and wait upon knowledge

Up steep and steeper heights
feet bare feel for every stone
but on they climb to the top
where they will sit silently in
days of prayerful patience
their path to this quest, minds
attuned to the inner ancient voice
that will reveal where the pink gems
lie sleeping, where they will find
them, waiting

THE BLACK CHERRY TREE

Standing there, it was so tall and
strong-looking it gave a feeling of
forever that our world was safe
especially to a small child who knew
nothing of trees or what they might
give us or what safe meant. But just
the same, the feeling told the truth

Special it was, standing at the very spot
where the car sharply turned in to my
grandparents' home, that magical place
where Thanksgiving and Christmas
happened

Like a solid soldier that one black cherry
tree had somehow escaped the enemy,
a growling road grader that widened country
roads, straightening them in curvy places,
and other things, reasons unknown

As a child will, awe of that tree carried
with it a belief the tree would always be there
and for a long time, it stayed put.

It stayed put long enough for me to
bury those special people, the ones I
thought would last with the tree

Maybe it transformed into a cherry cabinet
in a loving home, once more sturdy and
strong where hands touch it and feel
comforted by its presence or maybe
chopped to pieces by hands that did not
know the treasure it was and burned alive

DISCLOSURE

A moment to thrill
a half-moment to kill it,
an enemy's clever ways
always at work

Feeling the light
and sensing the darkness
of that half-moment
makes life questionable
and unbearable

like now when answers
are hard to give, answers
of childhood and long belief
in all that matters desert us

A baby, born perfect, healthy
and dead in two minutes
that half-moment when
a spinning world stops
at the most wrong point

and a vacuum pulls us inside
to be forever quandary-ridden
as drugged non-believers
with no truth or sanity

THE RIGHT TIME

They say "don't die in the dead
of winter," the ground's too hard
to shovel and people won't come

Hearing this a lifetime, it is easy
to see the logic, but very hard to
see how to manage it

The right time is when then? Seems
everyone would like the brightest
summer day when just the right
amount of breeze gives a pleasant
interlude of comfort
but is that fair to the dead where
comfort is earth-bound and
no longer matters at all?

When it's all said and done, what's to
be said and what can be done?
It seems philosophy of living or dying
serves little purpose at that moment
or the next

POSSIBILITIES

In the dead of night, possibilities, endless,
enchanting sparkle my thoughts so alive
with fairy Godmother's wand
until I believe them and their public relations spin
almost assures my mind that I can do it,
I can do and be all those things that
I have wanted to be and do even as age
goes faster and faster and time,
running at breakneck speed crooks a grin,
confidence has never been higher or more ill-placed
maybe if they had been so sure years ago
possibilities would be more than dust of sad dreams
as morning shines on them giving a quite different
view, sadly one with less bling

ONCE MORE

Having lived long enough to see
tender wildflowers come to life
again in mass factory ascension,
tulips budding and peach colored
roses raised from the dead, blooming
while there is still just barely
enough time to cover a body no longer
young but with sweetest memory
of childhood bounty made of feed sack
flowers and rickrack trim
sown perfectly only for one
by a grandmother's hand flying,
Wonder Woman on a treadle machine

Knowing

Night morning dusk cobwebs hang
lacelike above the land
holding onto the gray mat of
fierce memories
caught tight in the sinew of life
revisited

while time, tired of itself, seeks release from
dreams, scattered loves, lost hope of all
but just the same, wanted dead or alive
what reward should be offered?
what filmy truth, hunted down like
a bat hidden, will tell the tale?

in that classroom far far away
sits the student with all the answers
and from a distance she looks a lot like
the spider of me

THE UNBEQUEATHED

The house where all the memories were
is gone but always questions of why
did it have to end as it did fill the mind
but it has to be Mother's unwilling gift
her death gave the neighbor she did not
love that drives this day's unease
no remnant will be found where concrete
runs rampant as part of parking lot heaven
stretching life thin among bare goodbye whispers
and the words long said and so often heard
remind those who remember
"They'll never get it as long as I'm alive!"

WATERFALL

She said she didn't know why
her eyes watered but dabbing
tissues at them day and night
it always seemed there must be
a million reasons life gave her
knowing why is easier now as I
feel the water rising in me,
getting ready to spill out my eyes
like Grandma

1850-1914

A true story can never be topped by mere
chance or man's imperfect imaginings

So it was of the caretaker so long ago
who found his calling in caring for the
little country church in a place that was
just a spot in the road

his home was a tiny cabin on the grounds
where he found joy in toiling for the Lord

his blood was mixed by whom and how
was not known. That didn't bother folks
but the thing that upset some in the church
was the elaborate way he decorated the pulpit
for Sunday services!

The simple truth was he had a special gift and
deep love for the many flowers that grew on
the church grounds and tended them to beauty
as nature responded to his loving hands,
giving ever abundant, vibrant colors
to adorn the raised pulpit platform

from one end to the other, glorifying God
as the preacher preached

he was buried in the church yard he loved
so well, and a wonderfully, unexpected
thing happened. Upon only his grave, wild roses
began to grow, reaching across his resting place
arms of love like the pulpit he decorated and still
today they grow, beautiful and ever faithful
to the one who loved and cared for them
more than a century ago

CITY MICE

We went to live in the little house
we thought was big after all of us
were sandwiched at our grandparents'
after the war

We felt happy in our new home, it gave
us a different life, a life in the city full
of risky freedom, bits of Halloween scary
as we found our way along dark streets,
we knew our lives were changing
just not how much

Town water was bitter and for a while
they brought us sweet cistern water
to drink, but after a time we learned
to swallow the fluoride, chlorine-ridden
and God knows what else city water
while our DNA screamed in rebirth

WINTER

Winter is always nearer
than you think
like a train wide open
coming toward you
screaming louder and louder
clearly in control and
all you can do is feel
earth's faintest tremble
and you look more suspiciously
around you, did the wind just pick up?
Surely the sun isn't done
for the day and yet a feeling of
tomorrow coming takes over
every other thought

Not the Same

Funny how people tell you so many things
things you don't question at the time but later
when it crosses your life you have to think
about it

Take angels. We are brought up to think of
them as good celestial beings, but coming out
of afternoon slumber one showed up beside my
chair looking down at me and I knew the
somewhat see through blonde was just what I'd
been taught an angel would look like

Acknowledging her with a "hello Dear" she left,
her pale gold hair waving upward but I was
shook up and tried to make mortal sense
of why she had come to see me. I found no
answer, but I found her frightening in a way
I would never have imagined from all the stories
they told me in Sunday School

LELAND

If I had known you were on your way
coming as fast as your little heart could take you,
I would have stayed younger longer
so there would have been much more
time for us to grow older together
like we surely were meant to do
The fun times would have gone at a
slower pace and the sun would have
stayed longer in the heavens,
smiling on our innocent escapades
while laughter's music filled our
warm world of simple and wondrous
moments, love's lasting treasures,
if only I had known

About the Author

The author's lifelong natural love of writing and other creative expression started early, competing in local contests, as editor of her high school paper, and during college as a creative writer. A health career followed, managing Statewide medical review, and later as manager of physical rehabilitation programs, as well as in addictions and therapeutic mental health programs. Always ready to meet emerging challenges, she spearheaded grants and developed specialty programs to advance consumer access to quality health care services. A strong proactive drive to serve others achieve the best possible outcomes, especially those who are underserved and at risk in the community continued to passionately guide her work as a helping professional and community member.

A High-Spirited Woman is her first published poetry collection. It reflects her eclectic background and captures her compassionate spirit with the Universal audience. An enlightened colleague once recognized that, regardless of the job or its title, she works from inspiration. As a committed professional, she has been inspired by the courageous people around her who have allowed her the privilege of entering into their physical and emotional pain as they struggled to find stability and a new beginning in what is often for the recovering addict a hostile, unforgiving world.

She has walked beside them in the difficult journey as they fought to rebuild their life in the midst of great personal losses, uncertainty, including lost faith in themselves. These journeys opened a spiritual dimension pathway of enlightened compassion to understand the desperation of those who suffer life tragedies. Persons beginning recovery and treatment believe there is no hope to succeed because they know they have lost so much and that burden often overwhelms them. Encouraging them in their faithful journey to reclaim their life became a natural and forever priority and humbling experience.

A graduate of Indiana University, Bloomington with a Bachelor of Arts in sociology and psychology she received her Master's from the School of Social Work, University of Alabama at Tuscaloosa. She values greatly the artistic efforts of cultural expression in its many categories and treasures those who have shared their lives with her. She has lived and worked throughout the United States and makes her home in the truly enchanted land of New Mexico.

Made in the USA
Columbia, SC
22 August 2022

65072600R00076